THE CATBIRD
and other poems

Gerard Feeney

ISBN: 1456334263
ISBN-13: 9781456334260

In this flyover of a book, let the Catbird lead. As part of NATURE, it is also a "perching" bird, a friend to, in their SEASONS and MONTHS, PEOPLE, whom you should recognize along the way. As a relative of the mockingbird, the catbird mimics other feathery types with its own version of the comic, not in LIGHT VERSE, but, called the "Cat Thrush", it breaks out at any time in lyrical song.

TABLE OF CONTENTS

NATURE

The Catbird

The catbird summers at my place.
(Room with two baths,
Berry good meals,
R & R in the yard,
And a horn-of-plenty garden.)

From stone wall it mews
At me hoeing rows
Then touches down on a garden post
Turf-watching like a haughty host.

In fall, southward it will fly
After my grapes gratify.

As summer turns to sere
I should be upset,
Yet each year
The bird renews the lease,
And I yield to its caprice.

Flowering Dogwood

The tree in the center of the lawn,
in unsullied satin petals,
opens from its essence like a lover,
branches bursting
with too much whiteness for the trunk.

Its kin grows wild in the woods,
but squeezed by spring underbrush,
thinner, smaller, paler.

At night I note, from my bedroom window,
the tree's blossoms do not sleep
but glow, needing no moon.

Then heaven's sun unwraps the morning
in all its clearness, a limelight
on the lawn and that albescent tree.
Again, the month of May is a
world of white.

The Phoebe

The phoebe's not a bird of fame,
its only colors, gray and white.
Its song is like its name.
The female takes her flight

every spring, so far, to our place
where she will start her routine
using mud, moss and twigs to interlace
and take over like a reigning queen.

The bird will build a home beneath a bridge,
breezeway, or under outdoor lamps, too,
any overhang from which to catch a gnat or midge.
That's what nature wants these birds to do.

She makes her nest below our deck.
Now from the hawk or cat, she's free.
It's messy—but what the heck,
we'll let the phoebe be.

Luminosity

As in a child's picture book,
the sun faces up. It has a twinkle and wink, at first,
flicking for a spell on a hairline horizon
that is a stripe of light.

On this side of the globe, slow-motion morning
is a vaunting vision
that pushes out silvery night.
Animals rustle and begin to skip.
The great color wheel is about to do a spin.
Earth is still drowsy in sacred silence,
the seas kindle to glinting
and the day stretches.

Seas are no longer metal in first light,
which has snuffed out the hunched and reluctant
night.
Waves, in the curve of gold turning white, are blue.
Poplars begin their leafy prancing, swiveling in
scarlet.
Rays splinter the woodlands.

Now the honeyed center of the earth yields to the
white rush,
embracing and adoring the fire, water and air of it,
as shadows and windy places accede.

The wild vine finds its serpent tracks once more.
Gnarled old oaks show their lustral side.
Clouds roll and stream along the sky.
The sun becomes a clock against the void,
and every eastern being turns to sunrise and sea.
The planet tilts.
This is no time for moonbeams
It's the greatest light show on earth!

Dragonfly

As a child, this evil darning needle,
I was told, would sew me up,

this B-52 of insects,
with such a span, and sleek.

I was too young to notice
wings of amber
blue and green,
the *Violet Dancer.*

I could not know this strong flyer
ranges for miles,
feeds on mosquitoes, midges,
and keeps control—
now will land on my finger
and not sting.

What

made that bird, so famously red,
burst upon my window so
with such a thump
it flopped flat into a lump
on my driveway, dead.

When

I went to retrieve
it, fallen, and grieve
a bit, I had no need to mourn.
The creature'd gone.
It rose to fly live
and survive.

Why

oh why
does this recall
my once near fall
to death
on a mountain climb from earth to sky.
This memory, a quick afterpiece,
came in a breath
like the bird's release.

Lesson

Whatever could force us
to tend finite resources
and direct our wills
to stop oil spills
or put a freeze
on overfished seas—
the lesson is clear and strong and true.
Some things we cannot replace or undo.
There's a serious lesson in the bristlecone tree.
You must die a little, to live, you see.
It's not what we want, but what we need,
And important for mortals to aptly concede
to nature, and to its laws adhere.
It's such a privilege to be here.

Blue Lights

Viewed from a winter bridge
over a low loop of houses,
blue lights of TV sets
limn the snow.

In the twilighted empyrean,
nature's big living room,
the teal sky turns
to a wild indigo.
Rhythms past limit and knowing
hum high in sapphire,
pristine and notable.

Clouds

Pen me a poem on sky-stretched days.
Fly me to light uranic,
cerulean heights
where the air is more than anodyne,
a place of clouds pristine white,

perhaps lined with polished silver:
better, a nimbus of gold.
Or, of the opalescent kinds,
tinged with topaz, or
late from the searching sun,
lavender.

Show me skies of clouds
that sail and tumble,
have cadence of movement,
give soft auras off,
but crowd the ethereal too,
turn umbrageous, imprison the sun—
as lightning flares and thunder growls

Sing to me how clouds,
in a cataract of light,
out of some vast cosmic intent,
put a healing on,
calming us at the core.

Skyview

Who is there who has not heard
poets praise the sky,
big and rarefied,
vaulted, an inverted cup,
a tent of blue, a skylark's song,
the common bread of the eyes,
a thing to write on or find a pie in.

But scientists have accolades too.
What an atmosphere, this sky!
Meteorites fall against its membrane,
burning to nothing by friction;
and so, breathing for us,
remains the greatest work
of coaction in creation,
sure in size, perfect of function,
a diurnal miracle.

Stones

Not far from fenced-in Stonehenge's
prehistoric site,
in Avebury, children play pretend
on menhirs, dolmens and lintels,
a place neolithic too, 400 years older.

This does not remove the mystery
from these megalithic monuments.
We can date pottery, but not stones.
We are without names for leaders, tribes, people.

What were these stones for,
arranged in circles and rows?
Burial chambers, religious rites,
celebrations of the solstice?

Against hard-won fields, farmers
must have moved monoliths by miles
with logs, skins and many men.
Now the stones, in soundless gray,
rise from earth's bosom.

Our castles, domes,
Rushmore, *El Capitan*,
contrast with life before words began.
But the past is not petrified;

children climb on megaliths.
The stones are not so much winter deadness
as dearer for their mystery.
In their eternal silence
they speak of time's arrogance,
yet of space inside us.

THE SEASONS

The First Day of Spring

A backyard obsession is over.
The luncheonette for birds
under fingertips of fronting maples,
closes for the season.

No more feathery constellations
At bath and feeder.
No more the fustian scold of the bluejay.

Even in blank winter
birds give jittery energy:
A cardinal twins itself
in the little lake of birdbowl.
A Jay knocks harder than a woodpecker
at clotted bath ice.

The deviltry begins with
bullies—like wolves of the steppes.
Crows, squirrels and Tabby
prowl the perimeters
disturbing peace and plenty.
Something flashes, swift and feral.
A hawk claws a mourning dove, and flies away
Smaller wings watch in stoop-shouldered plumage.

But now, birds are in caucus.
A robin's chirrup, a crow's caw
become a morning chorus, an oratorio.
Mates will be chosen, areas limited, eggs hatched.
All will be here for summer bounty.

Let Summer Come

Let the sun warm seeds, move roots
make daisies drift and hollyhocks bow in beauty.
Let swallows swoop, sunbeams dance, country creeks
shine their silvery ribbons.

Let the sky unsheathe slow-motion clouds,
canopies of unbusy blue, white, gold,
the sun play shadowy stripes on walls and trees.

Let happenings, holidays, bugles and bells
begin with a lemonade haze
toward basking afternoon,
finish with an apricot sky
and a breeze for a mantra.

Let come the season of summer
transfiguring all in blessing
and light.
Summer: like a life that's long and rewarding.

I Heard Autumn

I heard autumn in the kitchen.
It tinkled the outdoor chimes,

then wracked the house
with a raucous blow—

one whole sheet of russet leaves,
a leviathan made of blur and brown,

rattling the window
erasing light and scumbling the spectral sky.

Intense, unforgiving,
in seconds, it clawed at the casement
became a vortex,
then clambered, humming to the housetop, swirling
        away out of sight,
            like some passing troupe in proud parade,
            or vaunting high god—

leaving my senses staggered
and my spirit to its own colors.

Let Winter Come

Let the junco veer through the andromeda,
then flit upward in an entrechat
while a chipmunk, on a wall, cocks an ear.
Let winter come.

Let robin prefer brown bath water,
squirrel leap limbs for a dogwood berry.
Late fall flares, but hurries the season.

Let leaves start and stop, dance around in a ring
or frost-crisped, blow through the yard
or scuffle the clasping ivy.
Let winter come.

Let creatures of nature take a whiff of earth
before the frigid snap, with air's bitter sting,
cracks, in tremolo. the wind-combed trees.

Let all hold their breath for first snow
for they've handled the northness, aren't caught by
surprise,
that white rush of season, the press of storm.
Let winter come.

PEOPLE

I Am

of the same body
that burbled in bareness

of tumbling games
while time was loose
bruised blue
toward prance and balance

of passion's fiery pleasure
heart beating in my ears
scarred with wrong, mortal hurt,
a piñata for life's troubles
but old enough always for spring
and circling love.

I am this vestment of the soul
the suchness of my body
unique and whole.
I am my body,
I am.

Small Child Running

Down a resort walk
A towhead child,
(with mother in hand,
father too), skips, trips, jumps toward
the summer place on the shore,

mostly running, running.

Two parents, only heart
apart from the walking cherishment
outside their bodies,

walk.

But small feet do not meet the other stride
so she runs and runs,
her heart beating to her short body's best.

"Keep your feet on the ground," they'd later say
in serious sounds.

She'd find,
falling behind –
the way of the world
is running
small with shortcoming
to whom she would be.

Lottery Player

He totters into his holy place
every morning, nose above the counter,
a mite of a man, all veins and knobbiness.

Amid pale smoke, being his own adventurer,
he chants his plainsong: "Power Ball."…"Play Four,"
not concerned with now, never an instant winner.

His is a wanting life from the hot center of hope.
He sees richness in risk.
Tamed minds do not know, as he does,
chance is the rhythm binding all men.

Sniggers will dissipate
when bugles and bells sound,
stars will quiver, he'll romp with the rich.
He'll wear a frock of gold,
be Puss in Boots, a terrible force of sudden luck.

The Strutter

On this livelong summer day
finally in full view
comes the marching band
with its whetted edge,
the drum major.

A frothy euphoria takes over,
each heart knocking, eyes riveted.
Here, Anytown, USA, becomes the heart of the
world.

The major is the tall one
nodding at bystanders,
his chest flickering medals, scintillant gems.
He struts to each side, stops for applause.

A performer now, he criss-crosses the pavement,
clicks his heels and wheels about with giddy pride.
The high step master of them all,
he goes the limits of the perimeter in emerging
orbits,
takes the baton and tosses an aerial.
The crowd gawks, caught in a permanent present.
Now no longer the whirling Sufi dancer,
he ends with a boogaloo.

The watchers leave the rhythm and rite of parade,
knowing who was in charge of the rightness of
things,
who, through the great arching motion of his strut,
before they go back to used-to-be,
gave them a symbol of confidence, a surfeit of glory.

Stripes

Here's to all things made of stripe,
Bass, zebras, lines of type.

On tigers, awnings, fancy ties,
Stripes find ways to mesmerize.

Forget wrought-iron gates or referees.
Stripes flow and wave with rhythmic ease.

Botticelli and Blake made "line" create.
They helped us to love all things striate.

The Eiffel and Gothic are surely art.
Yet the Guggenheim's strands are off the chart.

Even music sheets' lines with bars
Suggest the songs of spheres and stars.

So from Parthenon to picket fence,
Let us have stripes, their magnificence!

Emergencies

The room brims with humanity's
rumpled look of something having happened.

They sign in and wait, sign again and wait
sitting in a narrow deep trough of silence.

Parents grasp children
brave and naïve before the sewing-up.

The name-call is relief
and so the soft civilities of the nurse
before the doctor enters, all assurance, answers.

A boy is hooked by his own fishing lure.
Cupping his eye, a man walks feebly by.

Systems chart the run of blood,
the start of mending muscle, bone.

The hospital trees bud and thrive
in the spring sun.
While everyone plans to live their lives,
and can't.

The Unsupple

I am past my youthful arabesques
and somersaulting like a tumbleweed.

My stork legs I do not trust in undulating water.
Some think I'm the clumpy knob on a cane,
wooden-apple stiff,
beginning to look like the dead bones of trees.

But I am not all tooth and claw yet:

I crave the rhythm of the water's lap and roll.
In the green going
I want to wriggle and lace and strap,
to flex like my hungry eyes.
I am not rickety-ready for the final writhing.

I want to move like I'm loved all over,
to billow like a sail and follow the path of stars.

Caregiver

The sky opens, the road is straight.
It is summer when airs are kind.
Old toes dip into a lapping lake.
Winter gazes over the August day.

The caregiver resolutely eyes her people,
absorbs whatever their little lusters,
understands their fever
and fidgets with remembrance,
carrying the world's dead weight.

She yearns for the smile, a look,
the way light is the next good thing.
For hope can grow again in sun-aged faces
when she inspirits lithe laughter.

All sip and savor at the picnic table,
one-on-one, or in a cadenza of small talk.

For the caregiver, every day's packed with perhaps;
there is countryside, sea and the seasons.
It is Sandburg's "live long and laugh loud."

The old move in a whir of wheelchairs,
board for home,
led by their impresario,
she, lost in a victory of serving,
a crowd of herself, a synonym for love.

In Elmgrove

memorials remain
in vaults and mossy mausoleums.

An earthen puppy and pinwheel
mark a grave
that lies beside a Celtic cross
and family of five.

There's my next-door neighbors' plot,
yet unused, tombstones for two.

A lone stone bench sits over
where the Mystic flows widest
and wind turns a mobile in a monument.

Juncos wing in and out
of a feeder filled
for a bygone bird-lover.

Someone's left anew
an eternal lamp
and veteran's flag.

My crunch of graveled path
rises above the thrum of cars
on Route 95.

Death and life are one
in Elmgrove.

KA-CHING

Money
love's challenge,
gives the best free ride
with the planet's pleasures
or a neon name.
It glints with possibility,
a Joseph's coat,

but like death, is a source of anxiety,
a good servant, bad master,
the husk, not the kernel.

It plays pretend,
sates with quick profits,
prowls the perimeter of one's life.

Every other truth slides over
making room for its superior,
until the sound of ka-ching
cannot match the ka-boom of the heart
nor the singers of existence,

LIGHT VERSE

The Cubicle

They've moved me to a cubicle in order to save space.
I do corporate work and they've given me this place.

I am the white collar company worker.
In my cubicle, I can never be a shirker.

My office has no windows, nor has it any doors.
It's very claustrophobic, not at all like yours.

My back is to others in this syndicated maze.
I hanker for the office of the good old days.

The dividers of my space do not reach the ceiling.
They're too high to look over, not that all appealing.

Who might pass my entrance I can never really know,
They can listen to me on the phone. It's always touch
and go.

The boss—here or not—has the presence of a fossil.
So I feel I must always be obedient and docile.

You can't demand a change; you can't do much
protesting.
It's not good when they pass by and see that you are
resting.

There is no casual group, nor space to gossip at.
No water-cooler circle, no confidential chat.

I've promised myself the day I strike it rich,
I won't be in a cubicle when I find my niche.

Advice

Of all things naughty or nice,
If it's free, it must be advice.
When we ask advice, knowing the answer's "no"
Don't we really want a different one though?

Advice is given "for your sake,"
Yet like medicine, it's hard to take.
We ask for advice from friend or mate
But want it, in truth, to corroborate.

Rather than words with sage and spice–
A good scare's worth more than advice.
Advice is for those, after all has ceased,
who need it most, but like it least.

Those who give you advice are bores;
Except, of course, when they ask for yours.
If you give it to soothe some particular grief
Whatever you do, keep it brief.

Advice is all around and it's ample
The best is in the form of example.
The greatest appeal of advisors who make it,
Are in these words: "You don't have to take it."

Some good advice we like to re-tell.
Like "tip the breakfast waitperson well."
But let this poem advise <u>not</u> to advise,
And you will be healthy, wealthy and wise.

Island

I'd like an island
a just-in-case place
to know life in its pithy meanings,
be glad for long days and survival,
and boundaries that capture the soul.

I'd like a blessed Eden
away from war and woe,
safe and certain,
private, perfect,
with no guilt or grime.

Each brimming year,
I'd enjoy the wind on water,
the sapphire night and sweet air.
On this sunrisen isle,
there'd be a brambly forest,
high heartlands, green valleys,
a garden cosmos,
flowers bowing silent hosannas.
I'd hear all the good noises of living,
gather armfuls of summer
and watch the moon step down.

I'd have nectared leisure
to read ignited words,
grasp the gratuity of all that is,
know everything under the sun,
solve the mystery of the ordinary,
be equal to the gods.

But the clock chimes.
Your inscrutable smile sees
a cul-de-sac in my heart,
the thud of reality.

Who Knows the Toes?

I have a problem, it comes at night
as I accede to passing of light,
get into bed, at the day's close,
and, all comfy, stick out my toes.

When I was young I was told
that unless my toes, I did enfold,
in blankets and sheets and warming dreams,
I might meet monsters, bad as it seems.

I feared the fiend who'd get at my toes
before I could even start repose.
Now I'm through with that stuff and need not fret
'Cus I keep my toes in the bed—and yet

I will not put my toes out too long
knowing, of course, I'm completely wrong
to think, to dream, or ever suppose
some thing would dare bite my adult toes.

Each night I try to forget those days
of phantoms and demons and dragons ablaze
and keep my toes hidden within
the warmth and safety of the blanket I'm in.

I still can't prevent my curious intent
of sticking out feet, being indifferent,
but over me comes, from the top of my nose,
a chill that quivers the points of my toes

and swiftly I pull them into my bed
still bothered, a bit, by the awful dread
of the lurking beast that maybe chose
to come TONIGHT and nibble my toes.

They've Got Me Colored

Whatever happened to those colors three
the ones they called primary?

Did you read the latest clothing catalogs?
and the names they give to all those togs?

Last I heard, blue's still the color of sky and sea.
reminds us of temperance and sobriety.
Movies, moons and lagoons are blue.
There is yacht club and Alice and Prussian too.

But delft blue? A color named gourd? There has to
be hope
if you don't know colors of "oatmeal" or "taupe."

Yellow is sun, gold and desert parches,
butter, pencils and MacDonald's arches.
It's cowardice, evil and being ill.
old paper, speed bumps, a spring daffodil.

Red is anger, diamonds, hearts and debt.
or Satan as boiled crab as you can get.
It's war, sin and passion,
but it's "Cherub" and "Cayenne" in the clothing
fashion.

So what's it all to become?
Black not so sable, skies called "plum?"
Brownish pink called "nude": it's all attitude.

Of all this I won't get upset, or red. I think
instead, I'll be chic and become "bubble-gum pink."

THE MONTHS

January

Pewter skies, spirits and sun at a low.
Stygian nights and snow like a whipsaw.
The slate is cold, but clean.
Renewal starts in shards of sunglow
and what seed catalogs mean
as well as winter thaw.

January is Xanthippe stern,
the real
before the ideal.
Yet a sibyl of spring and return,
in its promise, we quest
again for the best.

February

In the short month, simple and fierce,
mornings are rimy,
colder air cracks the ice-edged pond,
the wind creases our faces,
contracting our throats.

It's enough to cause a snowed-in depression,
snug and safe, inside wall and woolen.

But like pioneers, we follow the sun.
The ice seems crystalline.
Bark and branch form a sleek geometry.
Shadows shift under the higher song of the sun.
Two minutes more of light each day.
February's a bagatelle.

Until a new snow.

Late March Snow

Now the underwood shows
cotton-puffs like a Georgia field.

Edgelines disappear
and the serenity of sun burns firmer.

Though there is not whiff of wind,
pines shake off snow like a wet dog.

Treetops unwrap their ermine.
The white carapace of winter fractures.

April

I know the words the poet spread.
"April is the cruelest month," he said.
Yes, everything seems bare and bleak
and chilly rain beats on your cheek.
It comes in time to tantalize
ere nature's colors greet the eyes.
Forsythias, daffodils don't match
with lawns that show each hole and patch.
Lilacs and maybush are blooms away.
The birds won't nest until it's May.

BUT...

It's easier to believe in spring
when you see the robin and redwing.
Ice is off river and it matters
that light laps dark and brook chatters.
Along dusty roads is bright celandine.
Its startling green is a seasonal sign.
Dandelions in yellow rosettes
have bloomed before coming violets.
With your feet on the ground, you feel that urge
for fingers in soil—and for spring to emerge.
But belief in spring and hoping things grow
is not needed now. You just simply know.

In May Month

lacy trees have long yielded to gladsome green
and flowers lean upon the air.

Now comes the ache of all unsaid of May.
A yeasty aura uncenters our mind from ourselves
to mayflower vibernum, a scent of paradise.

Lawns show golden stars of dandelions.
Everything is blossom-tufted.
Plants bud and burgeon,
blooms burst in garden, over gate,
more light slides through fences.
The weathering land is more accepting
to what buzzes, leaps and bites
amidst a floral waterfall.

Like growing May itself,
in silences and space,
we send out tendrils of attention.
We notice shafts of sunlight stronger.
Pussy willows have shed their gray fur.
Lilacs, heaven-sweet,
are in pyramids of purple curls.

May is in full regalia.

June

Heaven's big sun
shows months of hot frontiers to cross.
June, at the apogee of the year's arc,
full-throated, suffuses brightness
the way light arrives out of nothing.

It's as if the sun's luxury is not enough.
Nature opens the portals wide:
The sky is a blue expanse.
Air is more golden.
The forests become ferny.
We are in the greenwood.

People bathe, bronze and picnic.
Fish and frogs splash, insects sing.
Hummingbirds are at the hosta.
Roses and radishes blush.
Daisies lace the fields.
Rain, in showers, scents the vines.

The yeasty universe of summer is here,
thanks to what June does
to sinew and soul,
starting life up again.

July Summer

From the red-eyed morning haze
the demented summer
warms, swarms,
steams, a hot curry,
to sulfurous, molten light,
suffusing earth in umber.
The afternoon burns to a close,
vanishing in the vapor.
Serried in dark,
suspirers find respite
in the coda of a cotton-soft night.

August

In August,
time folds into the long moment.
Nature shows off its somnolence.
After the wan, lemony light of morning,
there is a hush of portent before the short days.

At first, on a flame-white disc, the sun swells blood red.
Morn catches fire.
A dictatorial sun, high and hot in a molten sky,
becomes noonday scalding.
Timbers crack, leaves snap in the heat-hazed day.
Nature is, no more, plain water and raw greens.
The summer's grown tired.

But with a drowsy, not leaden sleep,
the sun, that gives us life, will serve relief.
Before eve, its saffron will gild the meadows,
glint over pools and suffuse the seas.

September

September is closer to the brim.
Goodbyes and hellos for her and him.
Arriving and parting is something for all.
Bye to summer; Hi to fall.
The lifeguard's post stands discrete;
He's gone for ivy friends to meet.
First grade's for the six year old
Looking for mom's hand to hold.
At stations, bus, rail and air,
Parents' eyes glaze over, stare
At freshmen sons and daughters sent,
Wondering where the years went.

Ready for frost, September is not.
Morns turn cold, but noon is hot.
The moon is bright,
This autumn night.
Trees edge over in red, the grass in rime.
Here is mapped out merciless time.

The Providing Month

Give me October for the best moons of the year.
Its days bring all-at-onceness to autumn.

Giddy wild geese arrow south
in a snap of frigid air and cerulean sky.

October enrobes maples
in cerise and crimson,
sumacs in early scarlet.
Oaks go to antique gold, rich tans,
dogwoods to ruby-like berries

October is wood smoke, the tang of cider
and purple stain of wild grapes.
(The garden's in root cellar and pantry.)

At leaf-fall the world
becomes wider than field, higher than silo.
We think broad horizons, remote stars,
see things without strain.

The leaves will sodden with rain,
settle, protecting nuts and seeds,
become the humus for growth.

October is autumn in its beauty,
serene in the circle of time,
constant in change,
ripe and generous.

November

In November we elect, remember war,
give thanks, and are tested.

It is still autumn, but the flare is burning down.
Juices of life retreat to roots.
Animals scatter for shelter.
Insects burrow in and under.

Motley October is gone with the hiss of last leaves.
Skies fade to mauve and slate.
We too, withdraw to shelter and the solitary.

Low hovering clouds sheet the sky like bed linens.
Frosty air makes earth hard.
In the solace of our silence, ice is in the wind.

It is always the wind in this month.
Rainladen at first, gusty, then tormenting fields
and whipping the face, tyrannical and frigid.

A first snowflake flutters.
Snow is not prejudiced, coming now as well as
winter,
currents of it, whirling like a dervish dancer.

Winter, not calendar official, crouches in the distance
with its pale sun, brown pastures, white chaos of
snow,
its deep and dark sleep.

What to make of this diminishing, muted month?
Solitude will help us pass the test.

Dark Season

On this December morn
I watch the coming of day.
Sable night
is unforgiving darkness,
not that of shadow,
but cold, black air.

I step into frostiness,
silent as held breath.
Ravenous night
has taken all the light
into its cowl of winter.

Now ambient light silhouettes treetops.
Effulgent, layered, it blossoms softly.

Winter has deepened
in the gathering night,
petrifying nature.
Now time is more than an idea.